Stories Behind
Idioms 2

STEPHEN CURTIS

ACEL
Learning

© 2015 Acel Learning (S) Pte. Ltd.

First published 2015 by **Acel Learning (S) Pte. Ltd.**
18 Sin Ming Lane, #03-08, Midview City, Singapore 573960
Email: general@acel.com.sg
Website:http://www.acel.com.sg

ISBN 978 981 09 5312 6

Preface

Probably the most colourful and distinctive feature of any language is its idioms. This is certainly the case with English. Here you have a person 'biting the bullet'. There you have another person 'burying their head in the sand'. A little further on you find someone 'letting the cat out of the bag', while a woman is 'paying through the nose' and a whole crowd of people are shaking their heads over a 'white elephant'. It is all rather amusing and perhaps even a little mysterious.

'What is going on?' you may ask. You may equally well ask: 'Who thought up these peculiar sayings, and why?'

The books in this series do their best to answer both of these questions, but they concentrate particularly on the second.

It is not quite true that behind every idiom there is a story. It is not even entirely true that there is an explanation for every idiom – at least an explanation that language experts agree on. Experts quite often disagree about the origins of sayings; the origins of others are just too old and obscure to be discovered. But we do know where most idioms come from. We know the stories, the beliefs and the practices that gave rise to them. Those stories, beliefs and practices form the major subject of this book.

The author and publishers know that learning idioms can be a demanding task. They think that knowing the story or the facts behind an idiom will be an aid to learning it and to remembering its correct form. More than that, however, they believe that the stories and facts connected with the idioms dealt with here offer a fascinating insight into aspects of British and American history and culture. They hope that by the time you have finished reading the books in this series you will have learnt a lot, will feel more confident about using idioms in your spoken and written English and will have been frequently surprised and amused.

Contents

above board

What does it mean?

If something is done **above board**, it is done in an open, fair and honest way. In American English the expression is generally spelled as a single word, that is **aboveboard**.

- It was all fair and **above board**. Nobody tried to cheat.
- They were quite open and **aboveboard** about their intention to make as big a profit as possible.
- We were quite certain that they acted **above board** in all their dealings with us.

Did you know?

'Board' in this expression means a table. The particular type of table is one on which people can play cards. This sense of 'board' is no longer used in everyday speech and writing.

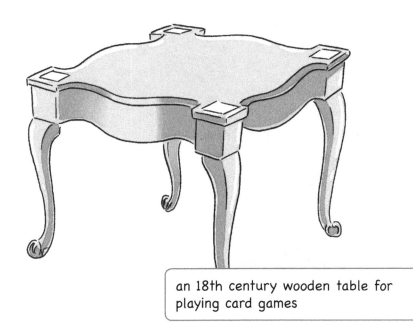

an 18th century wooden table for playing card games

6

Imagine you are one of a group of people sitting around a table playing cards.

You are probably playing for money, so you want to make sure the game is played fairly.

If someone's hands are below the table, there could be some kind of trickery.

But if everyone's hands are on top of the table, that is, if everything is 'above board', then you can be reasonably sure that no one is cheating.

apple of discord

What does it mean?

An **apple of discord** is something valuable or desirable that causes a quarrel because several people, groups or nations want to possess it.

- The island is an **apple of discord** for the two countries, who both claim it as their territory.
- I do not want this piece of property to become an **apple of discord** among my children after I die.

Did you know?

This expression goes back to a famous story from Greek mythology. It tells the origin of the long and terrible war between Greece and Troy described by the poet Homer.

The gods were holding a wedding feast. But the goddess of discord, Eris, had not been invited and she was very angry. She took a golden apple and wrote on it 'For the fairest' (that is, for the most beautiful goddess at the wedding). That was the 'apple of discord'. It caused many years of conflict among the gods and among humans.

the goddess of discord, Eris

8

Eris threw the golden apple into the party. Immediately three goddesses – Hera, the goddess of marriage, Athene, the goddess of wisdom, and Aphrodite, the goddess of love – each claimed to be 'the fairest'.

Paris, who was the son of the king of Troy, was asked to decide which of the goddesses was the most beautiful. The goddesses tried to bribe him. Hera offered him power; Athene offered him wisdom ...

... but Aphrodite offered him the most beautiful woman in the world. Paris gave Aphrodite the apple.

Aphrodite helped Paris to steal Helen, who was the most beautiful woman in the world, but was married to a Greek king. The king wanted Helen back. The war that followed lasted 10 years, and Hera and Athene, who were both angry that they had not been given the prize, helped the Greeks to win it.

at the end of your tether

What does it mean?

If you are **at the end of your tether**, you are so frustrated or angry or worried that you are about to lose your self-control and become really wild.

In American English, people often say that they are **at the end of their rope**.

- People have been coming to me all day and complaining. Frankly, I'm now **at the end of my tether**.
- We're all **at the end of our tether** and we need help now.
- I could sense that Joe was getting near **the end of his rope** and shouldn't be pushed any further.

Did you know?

A 'tether' is something such as a rope or a chain that prevents an animal from moving very far from the place in which it was left by its owner.

a horse that is tethered

Many animals are tethered to prevent them from straying, from harming themselves or from harming people.

This idiom is thought to come from the practice of tethering grazing animals such as cows or goats or horses.

The animal can eat all the grass in a circle around the pole to which it has been tethered.

But when it has eaten all the grass around the pole, it can get very frustrated at the end of its tether, trying to reach the grass that is further away.

blow hot and cold

What does it mean?

If someone **blows hot and cold** about something, they keep changing their mind about it. First they are enthusiastic about it, then they have doubts. First they are in favour of it, then they are against it.

- I thought Sarah was very much in favour of the idea. Now it seems she's **blowing hot and cold** about it.
- I don't know whether he loves me or not. He's **blowing hot and cold** at the moment.

Did you know?

This idiom comes originally from one of Aesop's fables usually known as *The Satyr and the Traveller*. A satyr is a creature from Greek mythology that is a mixture between a man and a goat. It has the upper body and face of a man, and the legs and lower body of a goat, as well as small horns and a goat's ears.

a satyr – a creature from Greek mythology that is a mixture between a man and a goat

A satyr met a traveller on a cold day. The man blew on his fingers. The satyr asked him why he did that. The man said he blew on his fingers to warm them as his hands were very cold.

The satyr invited the traveller to come to his house and get warm. He offered him a bowl of soup.

The soup was hot. The man blew on it. The satyr asked him why. The man said he blew on his soup to cool it.

The satyr immediately became very agitated. He ordered the traveller to leave his house at once. 'I cannot have anything to do with someone who can blow hot and cold with the same breath,' he said. For the satyr, being able to do two completely opposite things was a sure sign of dishonesty.

13

chance your arm

What does it mean?

If you **chance your arm**, you take a risk in the hope of achieving or gaining something worthwhile.

- I decided to **chance my arm** in spite of the risk of losing a lot of money.
- It was worth **chancing my arm** when the prize was something I had always wanted.

Did you know?

There are several explanations of where this idiom came from. Experts think it is most likely that this expression came from army slang.

A soldier's rank is often indicated by the stripes or badges worn on his arm. One punishment for soldiers who do wrong or make mistakes is to be reduced to a lower rank. Often the signs of high rank are ceremonially stripped from their uniform. If you **chanced your arm**, you did something wrong and you risked losing your rank if you were caught.

But Irish people suggest that the phrase has a more picturesque origin.

an army uniform with stripes on the sleeve

Two important Irish families, the Butlers and Fitzgeralds, had a serious quarrel, which led to fighting in the streets of Dublin. The Butlers were losing the fight. They took refuge in Dublin's cathedral, locked the door and refused to come out.

The leader of the Fitzgeralds wanted to make peace. He asked the Butlers to come out. They did not trust him and refused.

The leader of the Fitzgeralds had a hole cut in the door. He pushed his arm through the hole. He was **chancing his arm** because the Butlers could have cut it off.

Instead, the leader of the Butlers shook Fitzgerald's hand. The Butlers came out and the two families were able to solve their quarrel peacefully.

crocodile tears

What does it mean?

Crocodile tears are tears or expressions of sorrow that are insincere. If someone sheds **crocodile tears**, they pretend to regret something, but they are not really sorry about it at all.

- She wept **crocodile tears** over her rival's misfortune.
- How many people at the funeral were only shedding **crocodile tears**?

Did you know?

This is one of the many idioms that are based on an ancient belief about animal behaviour. Modern science has shown that crocodiles can produce tears. But these tears are simply a way of keeping their eyes clean and moist. They are not a sign of emotion, whether sincere or insincere.

crocodile tears

Crocodiles are ruthless hunters. They often hide just below the surface of the water near the bank of a river or lake. When an animal or human comes too close to the water, they leap up and seize them.

Travellers in ancient times reported that crocodiles would weep while they were eating their prey.

They thought that crocodiles did this in order to trick other animals into coming closer, so that they could catch them and eat them too.

Everyone now knows that crocodile tears are a myth. But the weeping crocodile is still a favourite image of hypocrisy.

I'm so sorry for taking your money.

curry favour

What does it mean?

If you **curry favour** with someone, you flatter them. You behave in an ingratiating way towards them in the hope that they will do things for you.

- She tried to **curry favour** with the director, hoping that he would give her a bigger part in the play.
- He's always looking for ways to **curry favour** with the voters.

Did you know?

The word 'curry', as used in this idiom, has nothing to do with Indian cooking. As people who are used to dealing with horses may know, to 'curry' a horse is to clean its coat by rubbing it with a 'curry comb'. A curry comb is a type of stiff brush.

The original form of this expression was *to curry Favel* or *curry Fauvel.* Fauvel was the name of a horse which was the 'hero' of a long French poem, written in the Middle Ages, called the *Romance of Fauvel.* Though called a romance, this was actually a satirical poem about the folly and corruption of the political and religious leaders of the time.

to clean a horse's coat with a curry comb

In this satirical poem, Fauvel is a horse which grows discontented with his stable. He goes to live in the best room in his master's house.

Fauvel gains a reputation for being very clever and cunning. Important people come to ask his advice, although what he mainly teaches them is how to lie and how to trick ordinary people.

People who want to gain Fauvel's favour try to please him by currying his coat.

In later centuries, people no longer knew who Fauvel was. They changed the idiom to its modern form.

19

cut and dried

What does it mean?

If something is **cut and dried**, it is already decided or settled and it is unlikely to be changed.

- I had the impression that the whole plan was **cut and dried**, and we were simply being asked to approve it.
- I believe we still have a chance of winning. The outcome is not as **cut and dried** as everyone thinks.
- She came with **cut-and-dried** opinions that we found it impossible to change.

Did you know?

Many origins have been suggested for this common expression. Some people trace it back to the preparation of timber. Wood has to be cut and dried before it is fit to be used. Others say that the phrase originates from meat that was cut into strips and dried so that travellers could take it on long journeys. The most generally accepted explanation, however, takes us back to shops that sold herbs.

meat that was cut into strips and dried on a wooden pole

Herbalists are people who sell herbs. Herbs are plants that can be used both in cooking and in medicine.

Herbalists traditionally would sell two kinds of herbs. They sold herbs that were freshly cut – cut in the herb garden on the same day that they were sold.

The other type of herbs was already cut and dried.

Herbs that were cut and dried would keep well. Most people thought that fresh herbs had a better flavour, however.

21

dog in the manger

What does it mean?

If you call someone a **dog in the manger**, you mean that they are a 'spoilsport'. They try to prevent other people from enjoying something even though they do not enjoy it themselves.

- Stop being a **dog in the manger**. You're not using the computer, so let your brother have a turn.
- I know you don't like this kind of music, but don't be a **dog in the manger** about it. The kids will enjoy it.
- I hate their **dog-in-the-manger** attitude to other people having fun.

Did you know?

A 'manger' is a rack or container with an open top in which farmers put hay for their animals to eat.

This idiom is another that comes from one of the fables by the Greek author Aesop.

a manger filled with hay

A dog went into a barn. It saw a manger full of hay. It thought it would be a comfortable place to sleep.

A hungry ox returned to the barn. It wanted to eat some of the hay that the farmer had left for it.

But the dog would not let the ox eat any of the hay. It barked at the ox and threatened to bite it if it came near.

The ox left the barn again, muttering.

face the music

What does it mean?

If you **face the music**, you accept any punishment or criticism for something that you have done.

- Sally had managed to cover up her mistakes on previous occasions. This time she knew she was going to have to **face the music**.
- We know there were other people involved, but Simon is the only one who has **faced the music** so far.

Did you know?

This expression first appeared in American English. Nobody is quite certain where the expression comes from. Some experts have suggested that the idiom comes from a punishment given to soldiers who had committed a serious offence. It is perhaps more likely, however, that this idiom comes from the theatre.

facing the music

In a traditional theatre, the orchestra plays in an orchestra pit directly in front of the stage.

Nervous performers would wait ...

... for the moment when they would have to go out and face the music. That is, they had to stand in front of the orchestra ...

... and the audience.

Practice 1

A Insert the correct word to complete the idiom.

1 a dog in the _____
   (a) box   **(b)** hay   **(c)** manger

2 to curry _____
   (a) behaviour   **(b)** favour   **(c)** flavour

3 an _____ of discord
   (a) apple   **(b)** fruit   **(c)** pear

4 to chance your _____
   (a) arm   **(b)** leg   **(c)** neck

5 to _____ the music
   (a) face   **(b)** play   **(c)** sing

B Match each expression in column **A** with its correct meaning from column **B**.

A	B
1 above board	insincere sorrow
2 cut and dried	keep changing your attitude to something
3 blow hot and cold	feel that you cannot bear something any more
4 crocodile tears	fair and honest
5 be at the end of your tether	already decided

C Choose the idiom that best fills the blank in the sentence.

1 When the election was announced, I decided to _____ and see whether anyone would vote for me.
   (a) blow hot and cold
   (b) chance my arm
   (c) face the music

2   The lawyer's job is to make sure that the election is carried out in a way that is fair and _____.
    (a) above board
    (b) cut and dried
    (c) at the end of his tether

3   Those are _____. I don't believe she's sorry at all.
    (a) apples of discord
    (b) crocodile tears
    (c) dogs in the manger

4   She tried to _____ with me by being extra nice to my little brother.
    (a) blow hot and cold
    (b) chance her arm
    (c) curry favour

5   The noise had been going on for two hours without a break and I was almost _____.
    (a) at the end of my tether
    (b) blowing hot and cold
    (c) a dog in the manger

D Each of the following sentences contains a mistake. Find the wrong word and replace it with the correct one.

1   Several people want this job and it could turn into an apple of despair among them.

2   She has been flowing hot and cold over this for several weeks. She must make up her mind.

3   He's being a hog in the manger and won't let us have the afternoon off to watch the procession.

4   The arrangements are shut and dried. It's too late to alter them.

5   John ought to be made to race the music. He's responsible for this mess.

fiddle while Rome burns

What does it mean?

If someone **fiddles while Rome burns**, they occupy themselves with trivial matters while some major event or catastrophe demands their attention.

- Scientists studying the probable effects of climate change have accused the government of **fiddling while Rome burns**.
- We're **fiddling while Rome is burning**. We need to take decisive action to deal with the crisis now!

Did you know?

This idiom is based on an incident in Roman history and the strange behaviour of a Roman emperor who many people thought was bad and mad.

'To fiddle' in this idiom means, primarily, 'to play the fiddle' (the 'fiddle' is an informal name for the violin). But there is another meaning of 'to fiddle', which is commoner in modern English. If you 'fiddle with' something, you touch it or adjust it without changing it very much or without a clear purpose. The idiom seems to refer to both senses at the same time.

The violin had not been invented in Roman times. If the Emperor did play a musical instrument during the Great Fire in Rome, it was probably a lyre.

lyre – a musical instrument

A great fire destroyed large areas of the city of Rome in the year 64 AD. Some historians claim that the emperor Nero was responsible for starting the fire. He wanted to clear land in order to build himself a new palace.

The same historians also claim that Nero watched the fire from a tower, while playing a lyre and singing a song about the destruction of the city of Troy at the end of the Trojan War.

Nero was certainly fond of playing the lyre. He entered music competitions which, because he was the emperor, he always won.

Other historians, however, say that it was just a rumour that Nero played his lyre while Rome burned. They say he actually directed efforts to fight the fire and allowed ordinary, homeless people to shelter in his palace.

flash in the pan

What does it mean?

A **flash in the pan** is something that appears promising. Its success, however, is only short-lived or it produces nothing of real value.

- Winning the competition was not the start of a great career, but merely a **flash in the pan**.
- Her continued success proves that last year's achievement was not a mere **flash in the pan**.

Did you know?

Various explanations have been put forward for this idiom. It has been suggested that the original **flash in the pan** was a trace of gold found by prospectors using large pans to look for the precious metal in river beds. In this instance, the prospectors were unlucky because the trace of gold did not lead to a major discovery.

Most experts believe, however, that this idiom comes from the unreliability of early firearms.

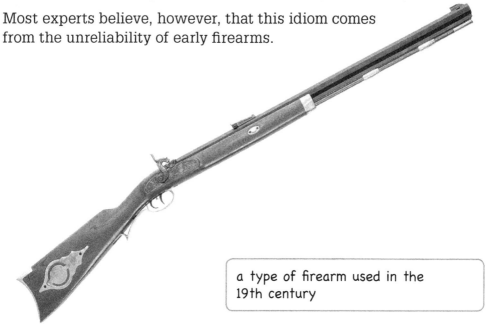

a type of firearm used in the 19th century

Old-fashioned rifles and pistols were fired by a mechanism known as a 'flintlock'. The flintlock was attached to the outside of the gun.

The explosive charge that fired the bullet and the bullet itself were rammed down the barrel of the gun.

The hammer held a flint. When you pulled the trigger, the flint in the hammer struck a piece of metal. This produced a spark that ignited a small amount of gunpowder held in the pan. The explosion in the pan set off the charge inside the gun and the bullet was fired.

But sometimes the gunpowder in the pan burned up without actually igniting the charge and firing the bullet. That was a flash in the pan.

give someone or something a wide berth

What does it mean?

If you **give someone** or **something a wide berth**, you try very hard to avoid them.

- I'd **give Sarah a wide berth**, if I were you. She's sure to try and borrow money from you.
- I **gave a wide berth** to schemes that promised to make me rich overnight.

Did you know?

The word 'berth' is a nautical term. Its more modern meaning is a place for a sailor to sleep. This idiom, however, uses an older meaning. It means 'sea room', which is an empty space at sea between a ship and another object.

to give the rubbish bin a wide berth

A ship or boat at anchor tends to swing on its anchor chain, pushed by the wind and the tide.

It is not good to pass too close, in case the ship swings and hits you.

It is much safer to give another boat a wide berth.

A skilful sailor will do the same for rocks and other obstacles at sea.

give someone carte blanche

What does it mean?

If you **give someone carte blanche**, you allow them to do as they like. For example, you allow them to take their own decisions and make their own arrangements.

If you **have** or **get carte blanche**, you get permission to do as you like.

- They **gave me carte blanche** to choose a colour scheme for the office.
- Lucy was **given carte blanche** to hire anyone she wanted for her team.
- We **have carte blanche** as to how we spend our budget.

Did you know?

Carte blanche is a French phrase. It means a white or blank piece of paper. As the paper is blank, you can write anything you like on it.

a blank piece of paper – you can write anything you like on it

The term **carte blanche** has a military origin. Like the white flag, it is connected with the act of surrendering.

If an army had suffered a very serious defeat, they would not be able to negotiate a surrender – they would have to surrender unconditionally.

As a sign that the victorious general could dictate the terms of the surrender, the defeated force would offer a blank sheet of paper.

The victorious general would decide what the defeated force had to do before he would accept their surrender. He would write his terms on the blank sheet.

15

go off at half-cock

What does it mean?

If something **goes off at half-cock**, it is a failure, usually because it was badly prepared or happened prematurely. An alternative form of this idiom, used especially in American English, is **to go off half-cocked**.

- It's better to wait until everyone's here and everyone's ready rather than to risk the event **going off at half-cock**.
- Brian's speech **went off at half-cock**. He obviously hadn't prepared it properly.
- The last attempt **went off half-cocked** because we didn't wait for the right weather conditions.

Did you know?

The 'cock' in this idiom is not a farmyard bird. It relates to the position of the hammer of a firearm.

A speech that is badly prepared risks going off at half-cock.

When the hammer of a gun is at full cock, it is able to fire immediately.

Some guns have a half-cock position. The hammer is pulled back part of the way.

This is supposed to be a safe position. Sometimes the hammer has to be at half-cock so that a gun can be loaded. The gun is not supposed to be able to fire with the hammer in this position.

But sometimes the mechanism does not work properly and the gun accidentally goes off at half-cock.

go to the dogs / go to pot

What does it mean?

If something **goes to the dogs** or **goes to pot**, it becomes much less good or effective than it was in the past.

- The country is **going to the dogs**. I'm not surprised that so many people are emigrating.
- I remember when this used to be a really nice area to live in, but the present residents have just let it **go to the dogs**.
- My aim has **gone to pot**. I can't even hit the target.
- That was before the business **went to pot** and started losing money.

Did you know?

These two idioms have a similar origin. Both relate to food that is no longer fit to be eaten as a proper dish.

His aim has gone to pot – he missed the target completely.

In former times, food that was no longer fit for human consumption ...

... would go to the dogs, that is, it would be fed to the dogs.

Similarly, left-over pieces of meat, bones and fat, and remains of former meals could go to the pot ...

... where they would be cooked up into soup for the following day.

have feet of clay

What does it mean?

If someone **has feet of clay** or is **an idol with feet of clay**, they appear to be very powerful or very virtuous and respectable. But they have a hidden flaw that makes them weak.

- Diana was devastated when she discovered that the man she idolized **had feet of clay**.
- He kept his **feet of clay** well hidden during his lifetime.
- This much admired institution turned out in the end to be **an idol with feet of clay**.

Did you know?

This idiom goes back to a book in the Bible that contains an account of the life and visions of Daniel, a Jew living in Babylon during the reign of King Nebuchadnezzar.

King Nebuchadnezzar – ruler of Babylon. During his reign (605 to 562 BC) his empire attained great glory.

King Nebuchadnezzar had a dream that troubled him. He called together all his wise men and asked them to explain the dream. But he would not tell them what the dream was. The wise men could not guess what the dream had been, so Nebuchadnezzar ordered that they should all be killed.

Daniel prayed to God for help. God sent Daniel a vision that revealed the king's dream.

The next day, Daniel told the king that he had dreamed of an image of a man with a head of gold, chest and arms of silver, stomach of brass, legs of iron and feet of iron mixed with clay. Then a huge rock shattered the statue's feet and the rest fell down and broke in pieces.

Daniel explained that the image represented various human kingdoms that would become progressively weaker. The rock represented the kingdom of God, which would overthrow them and remain forever. Nebuchadnezzar praised Daniel for his skill and made him one of the most important men in his kingdom.

have your work cut out

What does it mean?

If you **have your work cut out** to do something, you will only be able to do it with great difficulty and great effort.

- We shall **have our work cut out** to get the whole house clean before our guests arrive.
- I'm sure it's possible for them to do it, but they'll **have their work cut out**.

Did you know?

This idiom comes from the trade of tailoring, that is, of making clothes for people. Its meaning may seem rather strange. If someone else has already cut out the pieces of cloth needed to make a piece of clothing, doesn't that make the tailor's work easier rather than harder? The explanation is that the idiom has changed its meaning since its first appearance around 1600.

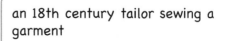

an 18th century tailor sewing a garment

In its original form, to **have all your work cut out** means that you were in a good position.

You were well prepared and well organized before you started work.

In later centuries the concept changed. The tailor now had assistants cutting out the work for him ...

... and giving him more than he could easily deal with.

in your element

What does it mean?

If you are **in your element**, you are in a situation where you feel comfortable and confident. You are doing something that you like and you are able to do it well.

- Sally's completely **in her element** when she's telling children stories.
- Give me a garden to work in and I'm **in my element**.

The idiom **out of your element** means the opposite to **in your element**. If you are **out of your element**, you feel uncomfortable, or you have to do something that you do not like doing.

- I feel **out of my element** when I have to make a speech in public.

Did you know?

This idiom goes back to the ancient meaning of the word 'element' and ancient ideas of what the world was made of.

Some people are completely in their element when they are with children.

The early philosophers and scientists believed that there were four elements in the universe: air, earth, fire and water. From these four elements, God made everything in the world.

Certain creatures lived in particular elements. Fish, for example, were at home in the water.

The natural element for birds was the air.

People were more complicated. Certain activities would be natural to certain people, as water was to fish and the air to birds.

20

Indian file

What does it mean?

If a group of people go somewhere in **Indian file**, they walk singly, one behind the other.

- The track was narrow and we had to proceed in **Indian file**.
- Julia led the way and the rest of us followed in **Indian file**.

Did you know?

The Indians referred to in this idiom are not people from India. They are Native Americans, the people formerly known as (American) Indians or Red Indians. This idiom, then, comes originally from the USA. It refers to the stealthy and cautious way in which Native American people moved through the country.

to walk in Indian file

Native American people were very good at tracking and hunting animals. But they knew that other people would be as good at tracking as they were.

If they were at war, they would want to stop their enemies from finding out where they were going and how many of them there were.

They would walk one behind the other. Each warrior would step in the footprints of the man ahead of him.

The final man in the line would cover the tracks made by the group. No one would know they had ever passed through that place.

Practice 2

A Insert the correct word to complete the idiom.

1 fiddle while _____ is burning
  (a) dome   **(b)** home   **(c)** Rome

2 give someone a wide _____
  (a) bath   **(b)** berth   **(c)** birth

3 go to the _____
  (a) cats   **(b)** dogs   **(c)** lions

4 have _____ of clay
  (a) ankles   **(b)** feet   **(c)** legs

5 have your work _____ out
  (a) cut   **(b)** put   **(c)** set

B Match each expression in column **A** with its correct meaning from column **B**.

A	B
1 a flash in the pan	have to make a great effort
2 give someone carte blanche	be ruined
3 go to pot	a failure that looks at first like a success
4 have your work cut out	doing what you like to do
5 in your element	allow someone to do as they like

C Choose the idiom that best fills the blank in the sentence.

1 We didn't interfere. We gave her _____ to choose the furniture for the office.
   (a) a wide berth
   (b) carte blanche
   (c) an Indian file

2 The show wasn't properly rehearsed and it _____.
   (a) fiddled while Rome was burning
   (b) flashed in the pan
   (c) went off at half-cock

3 They walked along _____.
   (a) in Indian file
   (b) in their element
   (c) with feet of clay

4 He seemed to be making a success of the business, but it was only _____.
   (a) a flash in the pan
   (b) an idol with feet of clay
   (c) an Indian file

5 Sophie is really _____ here. She was obviously born to be a teacher.
   (a) at half-cock
   (b) going to the dogs
   (c) in her element

D Each of the following sentences contains a mistake. Find the wrong word and replace it with the correct one.

1 The leader they so much admire is merely an idol with knees of clay.

2 War seems more and more likely, but our leaders muddle while Rome burns.

3 She will have her words cut out to achieve her ambition by the age of twenty.

4 I always give Harold a large berth when I see him in the street in case he asks me for money again.

5 I handed Sarah the money and told her she had carte blank to spend it as she liked.

keep your shirt on

What does it mean?

If you tell someone to **keep their shirt on**, you want them to calm down and not to get too angry.

- **Keep your shirt on**. He was only joking.
- **Keep your shirt on**; nobody's trying to cheat you.

This idiom also appears in the forms **keep your hair on** and **keep your wig on** with the same meaning.

- His wife was telling him to **keep his wig on**, but he was getting angrier and angrier.

Please keep your wig on!

If men are intending to have a fight with their fists, they need some freedom of movement.

Nowadays, they may well take their jackets off as a preliminary to a fight.

In former times – especially when the collars and cuffs of shirts were starched and stiff – men would remove their shirts too. Bare-knuckle boxers always fought without shirts.

If you could persuade someone not to take off their shirt, the argument could be settled peacefully.

kill the goose that lays the golden eggs

What does it mean?

If you **kill the goose that lays the golden eggs**, you destroy something that was providing a steady source of income.

- One sure way to **kill the goose that lays the golden eggs** is to quarrel with the person who provides your main financial support.
- They decided to change the recipe for their most popular drink and succeeded in **killing the goose that laid the golden eggs**.

Did you know?

Like many other idioms, this one comes from a story told by the Greek writer Aesop.

the goose that lays golden eggs

A farmer was overjoyed one day to find that one of his geese had laid an egg made of pure gold.

Every day the goose laid a golden egg. Gradually, the farmer grew rich.

But the farmer and his wife grew greedy. One golden egg a day was not enough. They thought there must be many golden eggs inside the goose and they wanted them all.

So they killed the goose and cut it open. But they found no golden eggs inside ... and now the goose was dead.

knock spots off

What does it mean?

If something or someone **knocks spots off** something or someone else, they are much better than the other thing.

- I thought Sarah's performance **knocked spots off** her sister's, to be honest.
- He didn't seem to be trying very hard, but he still **knocked spots off** everyone else in the competition.

Did you know?

The spots referred to in this idiom are not the kind of spots that are found on a leopard's coat nor on a person's skin. These spots are the symbols (hearts, clubs, diamonds and spades) printed on playing cards. But how do they get knocked off?

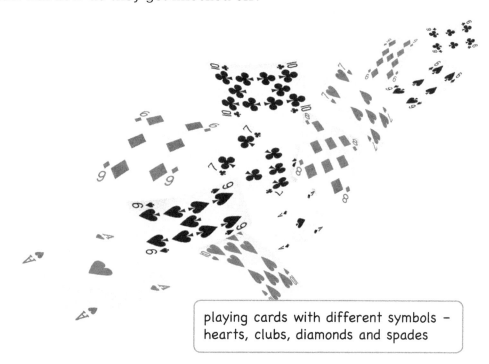

> playing cards with different symbols – hearts, clubs, diamonds and spades

Shooting galleries have long been a favourite at fairs and amusement parks.

In earlier times, playing cards were often used as targets.

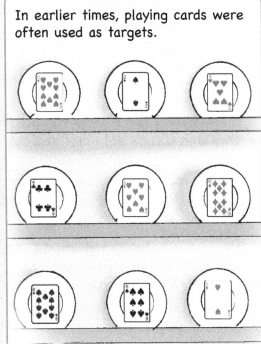

The idea was to hit the spots or symbols on the cards.

A good marksman could hit many more spots than his rivals. He would therefore knock spots off them.

know the ropes

What does it mean?

If you **know the ropes**, you are experienced or familiar with the way that things are done in a certain kind of activity.

- After about three weeks, the foreman thought that I **knew the ropes** and could do the job without supervision.
- It took her a long time to get to **know the ropes**, but she's all right now.

You can also **learn the ropes** or **show** or **teach someone the ropes**. These expressions once again refer to the knowledge required to do a particular job.

- It's not a very complicated job. You'll soon **learn the ropes**.
- The manager asked one of the senior saleswomen to **show me the ropes**.

Did you know?

The ropes referred to in this idiom probably belonged to a sailing ship. It is possible, however, that the ropes in question were attached to curtains and pieces of scenery in a theatre.

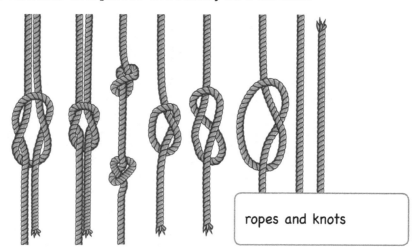

ropes and knots

An inexperienced person joining a sailing ship as a member of the crew had a lot to learn.

There were many different ropes on board the ship, and they all had different functions. They raised or lowered particular sails, for example.

It was easy to make a mistake until you knew the ropes.

And besides learning what different ropes did, you also had to learn to tie complicated knots.

leave someone high and dry

What does it mean?

If you **leave someone high and dry**, you abandon them in a difficult situation instead of helping them. If someone is (left) **high and dry**, they are in difficulties or helpless.

- The holiday company went bankrupt leaving its customers **high and dry**. Many of them had no money to pay their hotel bills.
- Poor families are often left **high and dry** if the breadwinner dies suddenly.

Did you know?

This idiom comes originally from the language of sailing and boats. A ship that is out of the water is 'high and dry' and cannot go anywhere unassisted.

to be left high and dry

Sailing can be difficult. A stretch of water may look perfectly safe at high tide.

But it may conceal a sandbank or a rock.

When the tide has gone out ...

... you could be left high and dry.

make hay

What does it mean?

If you **make hay**, you take advantage of an opportunity. It is often an opportunity that is provided by a weakness shown by something or someone or by a mistake that they make.

- If police officers ever went on strike, then the criminals would really **make hay**.
- The opposition was **making hay** with some statistics recently released by the Ministry of Health.

This idiom is closely linked to the proverb **make hay while the sun shines**, which is a warning to people that they should seize any favourable opportunity that presents itself. The proverb creates a link between the idea of making hay and the idea of an opportunity to do something in your own interest.

- I doubt whether the present situation will last for very long, so investors should **make hay while the sun shines**.

Did you know?

Both the proverb and the idiom come from the work done by farmers in previous centuries.

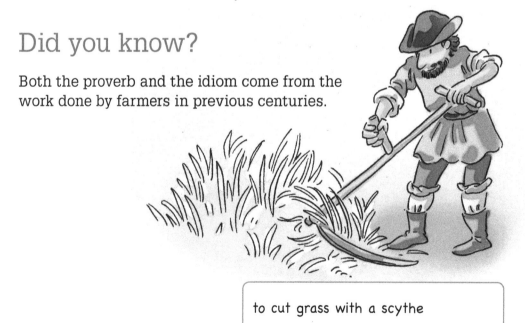

to cut grass with a scythe

Hay is dried grass that is used to feed animals during the winter.

The grass in a hay field is allowed to grow long. To **make hay**, you first have to cut the grass.

You then have to dry the hay. In former times, the hay would be left lying in the fields. Workers would turn the hay over with rakes so that it would dry thoroughly.

People needed sunny weather to cut and dry the hay and to load it onto carts so that it could be taken and stored. Haymaking was a summer activity in which men, women and children could take part, so it was often associated with enjoyment.

27

not worth the candle

What does it mean?

If you say that something is **not worth the candle** or **the game is not worth the candle**, you mean that the profit or enjoyment you get from an activity is not sufficient to balance the cost of the activity or the amount of effort involved in it.

- I calculated how much the additional work was likely to cost and decided that **the game was not worth the candle**.
- They soon realized that actions that brought so much international disapproval were simply **not worth the candle**.
- Are you sure that the plan is **worth the candle**? The risks are enormous.

Did you know?

This idiom goes back to the days before houses were lit by electricity. People often complain about their electricity bills nowadays. In earlier centuries, people complained about the cost of providing light for their activities as well. They used candles for lighting and candles were not cheap.

The idiom comes particularly from complaints made by gamblers in previous centuries.

Candles were used for lighting in earlier centuries before electricity was invented.

In the days before gas and electric light, houses were lit by candles, which were quite expensive.

A person hosting a game of cards might hope to win some money from the friends he was gambling with.

But if he didn't win any money ...

... then he might well decide that the game was not worth the cost of the candles that had been burned.

on the wagon

What does it mean?

If someone is **on the wagon**, they are not drinking alcohol.

- No beer for me, thanks. I'm **on the wagon**.
- Mary hasn't touched a drop since she went **on the wagon** about six months ago.

It is also possible to say that someone is **off the wagon** or has **fallen off the wagon**. This means that they have started drinking alcohol again after a period of abstaining from it.

- James was arrested for being drunk and disorderly after **falling off the wagon** in spectacular style.
- Should I offer Jane a drink? Is she **off the wagon** now?

Did you know?

When the phrase was first used (in America in the late 19th century), people said that someone was 'on the water cart' or 'on the water wagon'. This phrase was later shortened to **on the wagon**.

No beer for me, thanks. I'm on the wagon.

The unpaved streets of American towns could become very dusty in summer.

The water cart or water wagon did not carry drinking water. It carried water to scatter on the road in order to lay the dust.

Drunkenness was a great social problem in the late 19th century. People were encouraged to take a pledge not to drink alcohol.

Such people would say that they would rather drink the water from the water wagon than alcohol. That is generally supposed to be the origin of the phrase.

open a Pandora's box

What does it mean?

If you **open a Pandora's box**, you carry out an action that has many bad consequences that you do not foresee.

- The government is afraid that if it allows scientists to experiment with genetically modified crops, it will be **opening a Pandora's box**.
- I thought I was making an innocent remark, but I obviously **opened a Pandora's box**. I never expected Julia to react in the way that she did.

Did you know?

This idiom goes back to a story from Greek mythology. The story concerns the first woman created by the gods, whose name was Pandora.

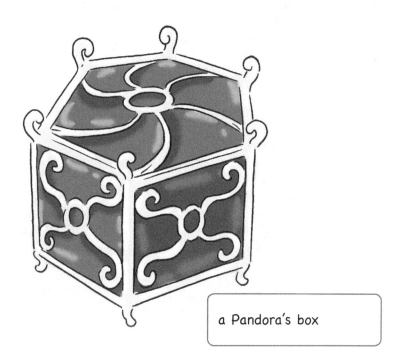

a Pandora's box

When Pandora was created, all the gods gave Pandora gifts. The king of the gods gave Pandora a box, but he also gave her strict orders that she must not open the box.

But Pandora was curious. She could not stop herself from opening the box.

All the bad things that could happen to people, such as illness, injury and death, had been concealed inside the box. They all flew out when Pandora opened it and began to make life sad and difficult for people.

When Pandora looked inside the box, there was only one thing left there. It was hope.

over a barrel

What does it mean?

If someone is **over a barrel**, they are in a very weak and vulnerable position. If you **have (got) them over a barrel**, they are helpless and you are in control.

- The hotel **had us over a barrel**. There were no other rooms available. We either paid their price or slept in the street.
- I hate the feeling of being **over a barrel**. I value freedom of choice above almost everything.

Did you know?

Most experts agree that this idiom comes originally from the language of sailors and seafaring. It dates back to the days when sailing ships would carry a lot of their supplies in large wooden barrels.

wooden barrels

A sailor has fallen overboard and is in danger of drowning.

His shipmates, fortunately, are able to rescue him in time.

He is in a very bad state when they get him back on board. They drape his body over a barrel, to allow the water to run out of his lungs.

While he is over the barrel, the man is completely helpless.

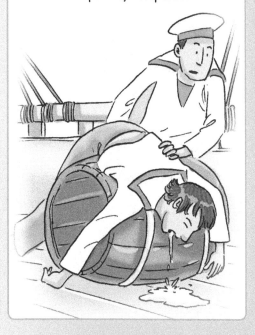

Practice 3

A Insert the correct word to complete the idiom.

1 leave _____ and dry
(a) high   (b) light   (c) low

2 keep your _____ on
(a) hat   (b) shirt   (c) shoes

3 open _____ box
(a) Pandora's   (b) Penelope's   (c) Persephone's

4 kill the _____ that lays the golden eggs
(a) cock   (b) goose   (c) hen

5 the game is not _____ the candle.
(a) for   (b) half   (c) worth

B Match each expression in column **A** with its correct meaning from column **B**.

A	B
1 knock spots off	abstain from alcoholic drinks
2 keep your shirt on	take full advantage of a situation
3 make hay	be able to make someone do what you want
4 be on the wagon	be much better than
5 have someone over a barrel	remain calm

C Choose the idiom that best fills the blank in the sentence.

1 The builders have told me how much the work would cost and, frankly, _____.
   (a) I must keep my shirt on
   (b) they have killed the goose that laid the golden eggs
   (c) the game is not worth the candle

2 The new car is absolutely wonderful. It _____ all its competitors.
   (a) knocks spots off
   (b) knows the ropes better than
   (c) is not worth the candle of

3 Lucy was a very good teacher and it wasn't long before _____.
   (a) I knew the ropes
   (b) I was on the wagon
   (c) I was over a barrel

4 He took all her money and _____.
   (a) knocked spots off her
   (b) laid a golden egg
   (c) left her high and dry

5 If Peter tells the police what he knows, I will surely go to jail. He has me _____.
   (a) in Pandora's box
   (b) on the wagon
   (c) over a barrel

D Each of the following sentences contains a mistake. Find the wrong word and replace it with the correct one.

1 Brian has killed the goose that fries the golden eggs.

2 When I started this job, it was Jean who showed me the strings.

3 I had been made high and dry when my business partner cheated me.

4 Keep your shirt off. I'm sure she didn't deliberately damage your car.

5 The situation may never be as favourable again. So we must make hay while the moon shines.

pass the buck

What does it mean?

If you **pass the buck**, you avoid taking the responsibility for something difficult or unpleasant, such as making a decision that is likely to be unpopular. Instead, you transfer the responsibility to another person.

- It was a decision that John really didn't want to make, so he tried to **pass the buck**.
- The boss has **passed the buck** to her deputy, who will probably pass it to me.
- I don't want any more **buck-passing**. People have to have the guts to take responsibility for their decisions.

Did you know?

This idiom originated among people playing the gambling game of poker. It became very popular especially among officials and bureaucrats. The US President Harry S. Truman famously had a sign on his desk that read 'The buck stops here'. This means that, as president, he was ultimately responsible for everything.

A buckhorn knife – the handle of such a knife is made from the horn of a buck.

The 'buck' in this expression was probably a knife with a handle made from the horn of a buck.

In games of poker, the buck was used as a token to show whose turn it was to deal the cards.

If a player did not wish to deal the cards when it was his turn ...

... he would pass the buck to the player sitting beside him.

pay the piper

What does it mean?

If you **pay the piper**, you face the consequences of your actions.

- Everyone's spending merrily today, but tomorrow we have to **pay the piper**.
- If you don't do the work now, you'll have to **pay the piper** when it's time for your exams.

Did you know?

This idiom most probably comes from the popular story of the Pied Piper of Hamelin.

Hamelin is a small town in northern Germany. In the Middle Ages, it suffered from a terrible plague of rats. The mayor and town council had no idea how to get rid of the rats, until a strange man in strange multicoloured clothing appeared. This man, the Pied Piper, offered to rid the town of rats in return for a sum of money. The mayor and council eagerly agreed.

the Pied Piper of Hamelin

The Piper played his pipe. The music charmed the rats. They all followed him down to the river and threw themselves into the water.

The Piper went back to the mayor and council and asked for the money they had promised him. But the mayor and council refused to pay.

The angry Piper went out into the street. This time he played on his pipe and charmed all the children in the town.

The Piper led the children up a hill outside the town. A cave opened in the hill. The Piper and the children disappeared inside and were never seen again.

pig in a poke

What does it mean?

A **pig in a poke** is something that you buy without examining it first. The idiom often occurs in the form **don't buy a pig in a poke**.

- A lot of people think that buying something off the Internet is like buying a **pig in a poke**.
- It's your own fault if you let them sell you a **pig in a poke**.

Did you know?

This idiom refers to a trick played by market traders at fairs in medieval England. The same trick is also the basis of the idiom 'to let the cat out of the bag'. A 'poke' in this phrase is a bag or sack.

a pig in a poke (sack)

In earlier times, a young pig was a much more valuable animal than a young cat or dog.

People would buy a young pig from a market or fair. They would fatten it up and kill and eat it later in the year.

It was common for the seller to put the pig in a bag so that the buyer could carry it home.

But if the buyer was not careful, the seller might cheat them by putting something else in the 'poke' instead of the pig.

show your true colours

What does it mean?

If you **show your true colours**, you show other people what you are really like. You reveal your true character to them.

- Everyone thought Barbara was really sweet-tempered and easy-going. But when she thought Emily was trying to steal her boyfriend, she **showed her true colours**.
- These people often only **show their true colours** when they are offered an easy way to make money.

Did you know?

This idiom has its origin in a tactic used by the captains of warships or pirate ships in previous centuries. The colours referred to in this expression are flags, specifically flags that identify ships and show which nation they belong to.

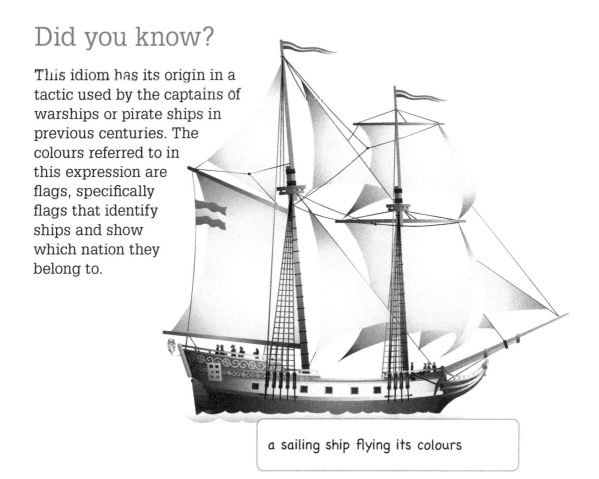

a sailing ship flying its colours

The most important flags flown on a ship would show which nation it belonged to. Sometimes a ship would 'sail under false colours'. It would fly the flag of a different nation from the one it belonged to.

The aim was to deceive other ships and gain an advantage in a battle.

At the crucial moment, the ship would show its true colours ...

... and begin an attack.

sour grapes

What does it mean?

The phrase **sour grapes** is a way of describing a person's negative attitude to something that they wanted but were unable to get. They pretend that they are not disappointed because the thing they wanted is not really very good or very valuable after all.

- Everyone knows Susan was desperate to go to university. If she's now saying that going to university is a waste of time, it's just **sour grapes**.
- Some of the complaints are simply **sour grapes** and can be ignored.

Did you know?

This is yet another idiom whose origin is a fable attributed to the Greek writer Aesop. The fable in this case is called *The Fox and the Grapes*.

a bunch of grapes

A hungry fox saw some grapes hanging on a vine.

He stood on his hind legs and stretched as high as he could, but he could not reach them.

He leapt up into the air, but the grapes were still too high for him.

As he walked away still hungry, the fox said to himself, 'I don't really care. I'm sure the grapes are sour anyway.'

strike while the iron is hot

What does it mean?

If you **strike while the iron is hot**, you do something at once, while you have a favourable opportunity. If you wait, the opportunity may be lost.

- The boss seems to be hinting that, if I apply for the job, I will get it. I think I should **strike while the iron is hot**.
- If we delayed, the enemy would have time to strengthen their defences. We had to **strike while the iron was hot**.

Did you know?

This is one of many idioms connected with work that was commonly done in previous centuries. It refers to the trade of a blacksmith, who made metal goods such as horseshoes.

a piece of metal being shaped into a horseshoe

A blacksmith worked in a workshop known as a 'forge'. It contained a furnace for heating metal.

The blacksmith would heat pieces of metal until they were red hot.

When the metal was heated, it became soft enough to be 'malleable'. In other words, it could be shaped by being struck with a hammer.

It was necessary to strike while iron was hot because as the metal cooled, it became harder again. The blacksmith would have to heat it in the furnace a second time before the work could be finished.

take something lying down

What does it mean?

If you **take something lying down**, you accept something, usually an insult or a setback, without trying to resist it or protest against it.

However, this expression is almost always used in the negative. When someone says that they **won't take something lying down**, they mean that they will protest about it or resist it.

- 'She keeps saying horrid things about me on Facebook.' – 'You**'re not going to take that lying down**, are you? Can't you report her to somebody?'
- They scored four goals against us in the first half, but we **didn't take it lying down**. From the first moment of the second half, we started attacking much more vigorously.

Did you know?

Someone who is lying down is obviously in a weak position. But this idiom probably comes from animal behaviour rather than human behaviour.

a dog lying down on its stomach

A group of animals, such as a pack of wolves or dogs, usually has a leader. The leader is usually the oldest and strongest male animal in the group.

If another animal stands up to the 'top dog', it might be threatening him or be about to attack him.

If the other animal is not prepared to fight ...

... it can show that it is not threatening the leader or challenging his supremacy by lying down.

the coast is clear

What does it mean?

When people say **the coast is clear**, they mean that they cannot see any danger and that someone can safely proceed to do something. Often **the coast is clear** means that there is nobody nearby or nobody who will observe what is happening.

- You can come out now, **the coast is clear**.
- We remained hidden until after dark. Then Susan went to check that **the coast was clear**.
- As soon as **the coast is clear**, we'll start unloading the van.

Did you know?

An idiom that mentions 'the coast' is bound to be connected with ships and sailing. In this case, the ships in question were not engaged in lawful trade. This phrase was first used by smugglers. Smugglers are people who try to avoid paying tax on goods that they bring in from foreign countries. Today, as in former times, the goods that people mainly try to smuggle into a country are tobacco and alcoholic drinks.

Make sure that the coast is clear!

The authorities in Britain knew that smuggling was going on and tried to catch the smugglers.

The smugglers, of course, did not want to be caught. They would bring their goods to a quiet beach.

They would expect a signal from the shore to tell them that there were no soldiers or government officials nearby.

If there were none – in other words, if the coast was clear – they could safely land their cargo.

39

the devil to pay

What does it mean?

If you say that there will be **the devil to pay** if something happens, you mean that there will be very unpleasant consequences for you.

- There'll be **the devil to pay**, if the newspapers ever get hold of this story.
- If that dog of yours bites a child, there'll be **the devil to pay**.

This idiom also occurs in the form **hell to pay**.

- When the captain found out we'd disobeyed orders, there was **hell to pay**.

Did you know?

It has been suggested that this idiom, like many others, originates from the language of sailors and sailing ships. A seam joining two planks near the waterline of a ship was known as 'the devil'. 'To pay' meant to cover a seam with tar. Putting tar on this seam low down on a ship's side would be a difficult task. However, most experts believe that the phrase has a different origin. In their view, 'the devil' is being used in its ordinary sense of 'the enemy of God and the embodiment of evil in the universe'.

the devil to pay

There were stories in the Middle Ages and the Renaissance of people who made bargains with the devil. The best-known concerned a discontented scholar and magician called Faust or Faustus.

Faust summoned the devil and offered to give the devil his soul in return for twenty-four years of pleasure, knowledge and power.

For twenty-four years, the devil kept his side of the bargain. Faust, with the devil's help, enjoyed superhuman powers.

But at the end of twenty-four years, Faust had to pay the devil what he owed.

the last straw

What does it mean?

If you say that something is **the last straw**, you mean that it is the thing that finally makes you lose your temper. Usually you have suffered a series of misfortunes or frustrations, but have succeeded in remaining calm. Then something else happens (which is **the last straw**) and you become really angry.

- When I lost all my data for the third time, it was **the last straw**. I took the laptop and threw it into the rubbish bin.
- Right, that's **the last straw**! I'm never going to speak to Charles again – ever!!!

Did you know?

This idiom is a shortened form of the proverb **It's the last straw that breaks the camel's back**. Some experts have suggested that this proverb also existed in the form **it is the last feather that breaks the horse's back**.

That's the last straw!

It is difficult to imagine a horse being loaded with feathers. Perhaps we should think of a horse being loaded with packs and someone adding a final feather.

It is easier to think of a camel being loaded with straw.

The camel is asked to carry more and more straw ...

... until the load is so heavy that adding one more straw makes it unbearable.

Practice 4

A Insert the correct word to complete the idiom.

1 pay the _____
   (a) devil   **(b)** pianist   **(c)** piper

2 show your true _____
   (a) colours   **(b)** flags   **(c)** nature

3 strike while the _____ is hot
   (a) hammer   **(b)** iron   **(c)** metal

4 take something _____ down
   (a) climbing   **(b)** lying   **(c)** sitting

5 the _____ straw
   (a) first   **(b)** heaviest   **(c)** last

B Match each expression in column **A** with its correct meaning from column **B**

A	B
1 to pass the buck	pretending you are not disappointed
2 a pig in a poke	there is nobody watching
3 sour grapes	to let someone else take responsibility
4 the coast is clear	serious consequences
5 the devil to pay	a purchase that you have not checked

C Choose the idiom that best fills the blank in the sentence.

1 I don't believe that Joanna doesn't care about losing. That's just _____.
   (a) a pig in a poke
   (b) sour grapes
   (c) the last straw

2 I feel as if Susan has just slapped me in the face. But I'm not going to _____.
   (a) pass the buck
   (b) show my true colours
   (c) take it lying down

3 There will be _____ if Janet ever finds out what we've done.
   (a) hell to pay
   (b) sour grapes
   (c) the last straw

4 Brian usually avoids having to _____ even when he's clearly to blame for what has happened.
   (a) take it lying down
   (b) pay the piper
   (c) pass the buck

5 It's really Lucy's responsibility to organize the trip, but she has _____ to Henry.
   (a) shown her true colours
   (b) passed the buck
   (c) cleared the coast

D Each of the following sentences contains a mistake. Find the wrong word and replace it with the correct one.

1 We only went out in the evening, after making sure that the cost was clear.

2 When Henry got home and opened the box, he found he had bought a pig in a pocket.

3 When Paula persuaded three of my best players to join her team, it was the lost straw.

4 Roger showed his blue colours when the enemy attacked our camp.

5 Don't delay. Strike while the iron is hit.

41

the wrong side of the tracks

What does it mean?

Especially in American English, if someone comes from, or was born on, **the wrong side of the tracks**, they come from a poor background or from among the lower social classes.

- Lucille was not ashamed to say that she grew up **on the wrong side of the tracks**.
- In the USA, even if you are born on **the wrong side of the tracks**, you can still aspire to own the railroad.

Did you know?

The tracks referred to in this idiom are the tracks of a railroad (or railway) line. The idiom goes back to the time from the middle to the end of the 19th century when railroads were being built across the territory of the United States and through its towns and cities.

Building of railway tracks in earlier centuries was done manually.

Every town in America wanted the good things brought by the railroads: swifter travel and greater opportunities for trade.

But people did not necessarily want the dirt and smoke and noise that went with railroad locomotives and wagons.

The prevailing wind tended to blow the smoke and dirt in one direction. Wealthier people built new houses upwind of the railroad. Poorer people were left with the less pleasant area.

The tracks consequently became a dividing line between the higher and lower social classes.

through thick and thin

What does it mean?

If you promise to stay with someone **through thick and thin**, you mean that you will be faithful to them whatever the circumstances and whatever difficulties or obstacles you may encounter together.

- They had vowed to stick together **through thick and thin**, and they had kept that vow.
- Genuine fans support their team **through thick and thin**.

Did you know?

This idiom originally had the form **through thicket and thin wood**. It refers to the kind of journey a traveller might have had to take in England many centuries ago.

fans who support their team through thick and thin

Centuries ago, large areas of England were covered in dense forests.

Any journey was likely to take you through the thicket, where trees and bushes grew closely together, and the thin wood, where they grew further apart.

There was danger in the thicket and the thin wood from wild beasts and bandits.

Later the forests were cut down and there was less danger walking through the forest. However, the idiom through thick and thin still meant being loyal to someone and sharing dangers and difficulties with them.

throw down the gauntlet

What does it mean?

If you **throw down the gauntlet** to someone, you challenge them to show that they are brave enough or skilled enough to do something, especially to fight, argue or compete with you.

- Acme has **thrown down the gauntlet** to other manufacturers by producing a machine that will sell for less than $200.
- The leader of the No campaign has **thrown down the gauntlet**. It is not yet clear, however, whether the leader of the Yes campaign will agree to a televised debate with her.

If you **take up** or **pick up the gauntlet**, you accept a challenge that someone has presented you with.

- If John **takes up the gauntlet**, we can expect a very exciting contest.

Did you know?

A **gauntlet** is a thick, heavy glove. Nowadays, gauntlets are worn mainly by motorcyclists or by workers who need to protect their hands. In earlier centuries, gauntlets were worn by knights as part of a suit or armour.

> Gauntlets were worn by knights in earlier centuries.

If you were a knight and another person insulted or dishonoured you, you had to fight with him to protect your honour.

Sir Ronald, you lie!

The way to issue a challenge to a fight was to throw one of your gauntlets down on the ground in front of the person who had insulted or dishonoured you.

If that person picked up your gauntlet, it meant that they accepted your challenge.

You and he would then fight, on foot or on horseback, until one of you surrendered or was killed.

toe the line

What does it mean?

If someone **toes the line**, they do what they have been ordered to do or are expected to do. This idiom, however, is more commonly used in a negative context. It is generally used to talk about the possibility that people may disobey orders or not do what is expected of them.

- Unless she learns to **toe the line**, she will not last very long in this organization.
- They have been threatened with disciplinary action if they do not **toe the line**.

Did you know?

'To toe' is an uncommon verb in English, which is seldom used outside this expression. It means 'to touch something with your toes'. There are two suggested origins for this expression, therefore two types of line that people's toes may have originally touched.

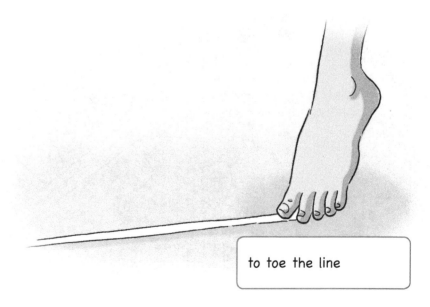

to toe the line

Someone who toes the line is showing discipline and respect for authority.

It is possible that soldiers on parade were the first people who had to toe the line.

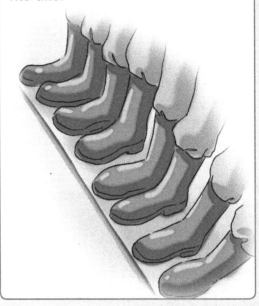

However, since a race is only fair if the runners all start from the same point ...

... the first people to toe the line may have been athletes.

45

Trojan horse

What does it mean?

A **Trojan horse** is a trick or a trap. It is something that appears to be useful or attractive or a gift. But it is in fact designed to undermine and destroy anyone who takes it.

- Some people suspected the group of being a **Trojan horse** that would eventually allow the militants to take over the movement.
- Have you considered the possibility that what looks like a valuable asset to the company might be a **Trojan horse**?

Did you know?

This idiom is based on one of the best-known stories in ancient Greek literature. It refers to a trick used by the Greeks to defeat the Trojans, capture their city and bring a war that had lasted ten years to an end.

'Trojan', as an adjective, means 'belonging to or connected with the city of Troy'.

In computing, a **Trojan horse** is a computer program that seems to perform a useful function but contains files that can carry out malicious operations such as destroying data.

the Trojan horse

The people of Troy woke up one morning to find that the Greeks, their enemies, had apparently fled. Their tents and boats had gone. All they had left behind was an enormous wooden horse.

Believing that the horse was a gift for the gods, the Trojans dragged it into their city.

But hidden inside the hollow belly of the horse were a few of the bravest Greek warriors. During the night they came out of the horse.

They opened the gates of Troy. The rest of the Greek army, who had only pretended to sail away, rushed in and destroyed the city.

turn a blind eye

What does it mean?

If you **turn a blind eye** to something that is wrong or illegal, you pretend that you have not noticed it.

- The manager is supposed to have **turned a blind eye** when members of staff stole small amounts of money from the till.
- I can't go on **turning a blind eye** to her mistakes. If she can't do better, she'll have to go.

Did you know?

The origin of this idiom is usually attributed to a particular incident involving one of Britain's greatest military heroes, Admiral Nelson. Nelson played a major role in several victories won by the Royal Navy during the Napoleonic Wars.

These were a series of wars fought between Britain and France in the final years of the 18th century and the early years of the 19th century. In his early career, Nelson was severely wounded twice. In one battle he lost his right arm; in another battle he lost the sight in his right eye.

Admiral Nelson - one of Britain's greatest military heroes

During the Battle of Copenhagen, Admiral Nelson led part of the British fleet to attack Danish warships in Copenhagen harbour.

The attack did not begin well. The senior admiral in command of the entire fleet sent a signal to Nelson to withdraw. Naval signals were sent by raising different flags.

But Nelson was convinced he could win. When he was told about the signal, he put his telescope to his blind eye.

Nelson continued the attack and was successful. Afterwards, the senior admiral forgave him for turning a blind eye to his order.

I really cannot see the signal.

turn tail

What does it mean?

If someone **turns tail**, they abandon a fight or refuse to fight, then turn around and run away.

- As soon as the police appeared on the scene, the men who had been fighting **turned tail** and fled.
- I was tempted to **turn tail**, but forced myself to stand my ground instead.

Did you know?

The origin of this idiom may seem obvious. An animal that feels threatened will usually turn around and show its tail to a predator as it runs away. Some animals, such as rabbits, have particularly conspicuous tails.

However, this expression in fact was first used in connection with the sport of falconry.

a falcon perched on its handler's hand

Falconry is a sport in which birds of prey are trained to hunt for their owners.

The falcons fly off and kill other small birds or small animals.

Sometimes, a falcon will refuse to fly or will catch up with another bird but not attack it.

A falcon that does this is said 'to turn tail'. Surprisingly, therefore, it was the hunter that originally turned tail rather than an animal that was being hunted.

wear your heart on your sleeve

What does it mean?

If you **wear your heart on your sleeve**, you do not attempt to hide your feelings. You make it very clear to everyone how you feel.

- Robert seems to have no secrets. He **wears his heart on his sleeve**.
- People sometimes make fun of Lucy for being naïve and always **wearing her heart on her sleeve**.
- Part of growing up is learning not to **wear your heart on your sleeve**.

Did you know?

This idiom first appeared in the play *Othello* by William Shakespeare. But the origin of the phrase probably goes back further than Shakespeare.

to wear your heart on your sleeve

In the Middle Ages, the tournament was a popular form of entertainment. Knights would fight with one another to show their skill and courage.

Knights would often say that they were fighting for a particular lady ... to show that she was more beautiful or more virtuous than other ladies or because they were in love with her.

Frequently, a lady would give a knight a 'favour' in return for his love or support. The favour was often a scarf or a ribbon.

The knight would wear the favour on his sleeve during the fight, which made it clear which lady he was attached to.

wild goose chase

What does it mean?

A **wild goose chase** is a journey that leads nowhere or an attempt to find something that produces no result.

- It did not take me long to realize that we were on a **wild goose chase**. The treasure we were trying to find probably did not exist.
- She sent us on a **wild goose chase** looking for a bookshop that she thought she had visited ten years before.

Did you know?

There are two possible ways to interpret this expression. You might think it refers to a wild chase after a (domesticated) goose or a chase after a wild goose.

The second interpretation is the correct one, and the phrase is sometimes spelt with a hyphen to make this clear: *a wild-goose chase*.

You might expect the idiom to be based on the difficulty of hunting and catching wild geese. But most experts suggest that its origin is rather different.

a wild goose chase

110

When they fly, wild geese usually follow a leader in formation.

In the 16th century, 'a wild goose chase' was a type of horse race in which one horse and rider were the leader.

The other horses had to follow the leader at set intervals, rather like a group of wild geese in flight.

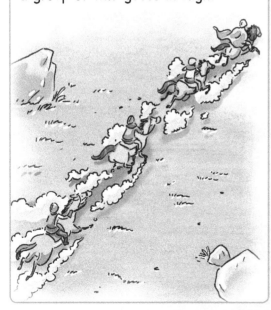

The leader could go in any direction. Taking an erratic course made the race more fun – but also more exciting – for the riders who were following.

with flying colours

What does it mean?

If you do something, such as pass a test or an exam, **with flying colours**, you do it very successfully.

- Joanna had been very worried about her history exam, but in the end she passed **with flying colours**.
- An experience of that kind is a real test of a person's character. I'm glad to say that your son came through it **with flying colours**.

Did you know?

The 'colours' referred to in this idiom, as in the expression **show your true colours**, are flags flown by a ship to identify itself and show which nation it belonged to. When you 'fly' a flag, you display it from a flagpole.

When you 'fly' a flag, you display it from a flagpole.

In a sea battle, a ship that wanted to surrender would 'strike its colours'. In other words, it would take down its national flag.

A ship with its flag still flying had not surrendered.

A ship that had won a victory at sea would return to port with its national colours flying proudly.

It would probably display a lot of other flags too.

Practice 5

A Insert the correct word to complete the idiom.

1 the _____ side of the tracks
   (a) far   **(b)** windy   **(c)** wrong

2 through _____ and thin
   (a) fat   **(b)** thick   **(c)** wide

3 throw _____ the gauntlet
   (a) away   **(b)** down   **(c)** in

4 Wear your heart on your _____
   (a) sleeve   **(b)** jacket   **(c)** coat

5 with _____ colours
   (a) fleeing   **(b)** flying   **(c)** floating

B Match each expression in column **A** with its correct meaning from column **B**.

A	B
1 a Trojan horse	to show exactly what you are feeling
2 to toe the line	to run away from a fight
3 to turn tail	with great success
4 to wear your heart on your sleeve	a trap to destroy someone or something
5 with flying colours	to do what you are told

C Choose the idiom that best fills the blank in the sentence.

1 The police knew what was going on in that house but _____ to it.
   (a) threw down the gauntlet
   (b) toed the line
   (c) turned a blind eye

2 The leader knew that her loyal followers would stay with her _____.
   (a) through thick and thin
   (b) wearing their hearts on their sleeves
   (c) with flying colours

3 James knows that he will have to _____ or he will lose his job.
   (a) go on a wild goose chase
   (b) toe the line
   (c) turn tail

4 Jean had a difficult start in life because she was born _____.
   (a) on the wrong side of the tracks
   (b) with her heart on her sleeve
   (c) with flying colours

5 There is no such house as 999 Acacia Avenue. We _____.
   (a) toed the line
   (b) were sent on a wild goose chase
   (c) turned tail

D Each of the following sentences contains a mistake. Find the wrong word and replace it with the correct one.

1 The company was a Trojan house. A lot of people lost a lot of money because of it.

2 Brian was so nervous that, instead of going in for the interview, he turned table and fled.

3 Angela passed her pilot's exam with flying wings.

4 Of course Diana knows that John is in love with her. He wears his harp on his sleeve.

5 People gave us different directions and we went all over town on a wild geese chase.

Answers

PRACTICE 1

A

1	c	2	b	3	a
4	a	5	a		

B

1   above board – fair and honest
2   cut and dried – already decided
3   blow hot and cold – keep changing your attitude to something
4   crocodile tears – insincere sorrow
5   be at the end of your tether – feel that you cannot bear something any more

C

1	b	2	a	3	b
4	c	5	a		

D

1   Several people want this job and it could turn into an apple of ~~despair~~/**discord** among them.
2   She has been ~~flowing~~/**blowing** hot and cold over this for several weeks. She must make up her mind.
3   He's being a ~~hog~~/**dog** in the manger and won't let us have the afternoon off to watch the procession.
4   The arrangements are ~~shut~~/**cut** and dried. It's too late to alter them.
5   John ought to be made to ~~race~~/**face** the music. He's responsible for this mess.

PRACTICE 2

A

1	c	2	b	3	b
4	b	5	a		

B

1   a flash in the pan – a failure that looks at first like a success
2   give someone carte blanche – allow someone to do as they like
3   go to pot – be ruined
4   have your work cut out – have to make a great effort
5   in your element – doing what you like to do

C

1	b	2	c	3	a
4	a	5	c		

D

1   The leader they so much admire is merely an idol with ~~knees~~/**feet** of clay.
2   War seems more and more likely, but our leaders ~~muddle~~/**fiddle** while Rome burns.
3   She will have her ~~words~~/**work** cut out to achieve her ambition by the age of twenty.
4   I always give Harold a ~~large~~/**wide** berth when I see him in the street in case he asks me for money again.
5   I handed Sarah the money and told her she had carte ~~blank~~/**blanche** to spend it as she liked.

PRACTICE 3

A

1	a	2	b	3	a
4	b	5	c		

B

1   knock spots off – be much better than
2   keep your shirt on – remain calm
3   make hay – take full advantage of a situation
4   be on the wagon – abstain from alcoholic drinks

5   have someone over a barrel – be able to make someone do what you want

C

1	c	2	a	3	a
4	c	5	c		

D

1   Brian has killed the goose that ~~fries~~/**lays** the golden eggs.

2   When I started this job, it was Jean who showed me the ~~strings~~/**ropes**.

3   I had been ~~made~~/**left** high and dry when my business partner cheated me.

4   Keep your shirt ~~off~~/**on**. I'm sure she didn't deliberately damage your car.

5   The situation may never be as favourable again. So we must make hay while the ~~moon~~/**sun** shines.

PRACTICE 4

A

1	c	2	a	3	b
4	b	5	c		

B

1   to pass the buck – to let someone else take responsibility

2   a pig in a poke – a purchase that you have not checked

3   sour grapes – pretending you are not disappointed

4   the coast is clear – there is nobody watching

5   the devil to pay – serious consequences

C

1	b	2	c	3	a
4	b	5	b		

D

1   We only went out in the evening, after making sure that the ~~cost~~/**coast** was clear.

2   When Henry got home and opened the box, he found he had bought a pig in a ~~pocket~~/**poke**.

3   When Paula persuaded three of my best players to join her team, it was the ~~lost~~/**last** straw.

4   Roger showed his ~~blue~~/**true** colours when the enemy attacked our camp.

5   Don't delay. Strike while the iron is ~~hit~~/**hot**.

PRACTICE 5

A

1	c	2	b	3	b
4	a	5	b		

B

1   a Trojan horse – a trap to destroy someone or something

2   to toe the line – to do what you are told

3   to turn tail – to run away from a fight

4   to wear your heart on your sleeve – to show exactly what you are feeling

5   with flying colours – with great success

C

1	c	2	a	3	b
4	a	5	b		

D

1   The company was a Trojan ~~house~~/**horse**. A lot of people lost a lot of money because of it.

2   Brian was so nervous that, instead of going in for the interview, he turned ~~table~~/**tail** and fled.

3   Angela passed her pilot's exam with flying ~~wings~~/**colours**.

4   Of course Diana knows that John is in love with her. He wears his ~~harp~~/**heart** on his sleeve.

5   People gave us different directions and we went all over town on a wild ~~geese~~/**goose** chase.

Photo credits

We would like to express our thanks to the following for the use of their images in this book.

p20 © siwasasil/Shutterstock.com; p28 © koya979/Shutterstock.com; p30 © Kletr/Shutterstock.com; p31 *top left* © mj007/Shutterstock.com; p45 *top left* © Kateryna Moiseyenko/Shutterstock.com; p54 © serg_dibrova/Shutterstock.com; p56 © Michael Schoppe | 8mb.de/Shutterstock.com; p62 © Aksenova Natalya/Shutterstock.com; p68 © Oleksii Iezhov/Shutterstock.com; p78 © elmm/Shutterstock.com; p80 © EV-DA/Shutterstock.com; p82 © Alexander Tihonov/Shutterstock.com; p84 © cynoclub/Shutterstock.com; p98 © Alexey Zaytsev/Shutterstock.com; p102 © George W. Bailey/Shutterstock.com; p104 Lord Horatio Nelson, by John Hoppner, The Bridgeman Art Library, Object 285890; p106 © schafar/Shutterstock.com; p112 © Jiri Flogel/Shutterstock.com.

Every effort has been made to trace the copyright holders of material used in this book. If any copyright holder has been overlooked, we should be pleased to make any necessary arrangements at the first opportunity.

Other books in the *Connect!* series

Connect! provides a link between language and culture. Culture has often played an important part in language development. In order to acquire a deeper understanding of a language, it is helpful to know the cultural context. *Connect!* aims to provide that link – in a light-hearted and reader-friendly way.

Stories Behind Idioms 1
ISBN: 978-981-09-5311-9

This first book of Stories Behind Idioms presents 50 idioms, focusing on where the idioms come from, what are the stories, the beliefs and the practices that gave rise to them, and how the idioms are used. Knowing the story or the facts behind an idiom will help learners in understanding and remembering it.

Amazing Western Culture
ISBN: 978-981-09-4725-5

Enter a world containing strange, unearthly creatures, as well as animals and ordinary household things to gain an insight into Western beliefs and values. An understanding of Western culture will, undoubtedly, help learners acquire a firmer grip on the English language.

For enquiries, please email general@acel.com.sg. *Or*

Visit us at http://www.acel.com.sg to find out more.

Chinese Characters Alive 1
ISBN: 978-981-09-2602-1

Chinese Characters Alive 2
ISBN: 978-981-09-2603-8

This light-hearted and highly illustrated series of two books presents 128 common Chinese characters and their cultural context. These characters are all radicals. Most of them can be used on their own, in addition to being components in word formation.

Written in English, this series will help non-native speakers of the Chinese language learn Chinese characters with ease and better understand the Chinese mind.

For enquiries, please email general@acel.com.sg. *Or*

Visit us at http://www.acel.com.sg to find out more.

CPSIA information can be obtained
at www.ICGtesting.com
Printed in the USA
BVHW011325150620
581343BV00015B/3